Lessons on
LEADERSHIP
and business

Adrian Geering PhD, MCC, CHIC

First Published 2007

© Adrian Geering 2007
Published by 100x Publishing
PO Box 320, Unley, SA 5061, Australia
www.secretsofceos.com

All rights reserved. No part of this book may be reproduced or transmitted in any form by any means, electronic or mechanical, including photocopying, recording or by any information storage or retrieval system, without prior permission in writing from the publisher. The Australian Copyright Act 1968 (the Act) allows a maximum of one chapter or 10 per cent of the book, whichever is the greater, to be photocopied by any educational institution for its educational purposes provided that the educational institution (or body that administers it) has given a remuneration notice to Copyright Agency Limited (CAL) under the Act.

National Library of Australia Cataloguing-in-Publication Data:
Geering, Adrian D. (Adrian Douglas).
Lessons on leadership and business.

ISBN 9780980339710 (pbk.)
10 9 8 7 6 5 4 3 2

1. Leadership - Australia - Quotations, maxims, etc. 2. Leadership - Quotations, maxims, etc. 3. Business - Quotations, maxims, etc. I. Title.

658.4092

Project managed by Messenger Publishing

To all the CEOs who accepted the invitation to join me in the great adventure of learning through involvement in The Executive Connection, Michael Gerber's E-Myth Mastery program and mentoring and coaching through Geering Solutions.

Thank you for trusting me and taking the risk of venturing on the most interesting journey in the world – the experience of being mentored and coached one-to-one and in a peer group.

Thank you for being co-learners in this journey of transformation and discovery and allowing me the privilege of working with your sacred lives.

You will forever have a place in my heart!

Your most valuable asset is your life and your most valuable opportunity is personal learning – personal development with great application. Your income will grow to the extent that you do …

Adrian Geering

> Keep thinking about your competitive edge. How do you keep your business fresh, alive and relevant to customers.
>
> *Karen Raffen*

your competitive edge.
business fresh value

Take responsibility in business. When necessary, be bold and courageous, taking a stand for what is true and right. If that means sacking a senior manager, do it.

Doug Brown

Don't fear change. Instead, embrace new technologies, business patterns and shifting cultures to find new and improved ways of doing business.

Andrew Downs

The brand is the only asset a business really has, so nurture it and guard it with your life.

Joe Grilli

> Leadership means personal cost. Be prepared to pay the cost; otherwise don't put yourself in a leadership position.
>
> *Nigel McBride*

Always move forward, even when you are retreating.
Mike Rungie

Focus on health, happiness and wealth – and in that order.

Roger Drake

What you tolerate, you teach.
Kim Scott

Develop your vision through intuition. Travel extensively, scouring the globe for new ideas, technologies and best practices.

Anthony Coop

> Authentic enthusiasm is the greatest motivator a leader has.
>
> *Glen Simpson*

Calm seas don't make good sailors. You've got to go through the wilderness to get to the promised land!

Bob Day

When moving on, do it decisively.
Burn your bridges and go.
Chris Stathy

Allow time for creativity.
John Chataway

> Grow by 15 per cent every year – without fail. This will then double your business every five years.
>
> *Frances Guzett*

Spend capital slowly – there's always tomorrow.

John Angove

> Be flexible. Realise that one size doesn't fit all and you will need varied processes.
>
> *Ian Stirling*

Don't assume other people know or understand your business.
Richard Hamood

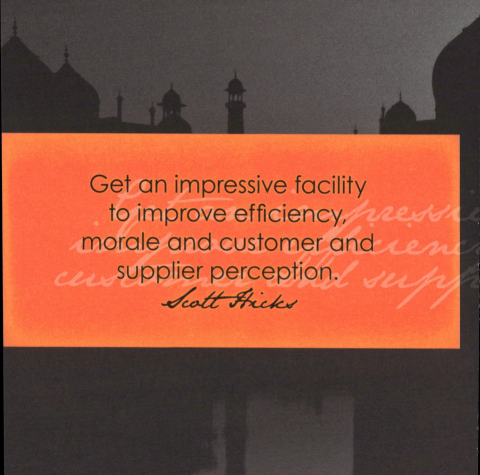

Focus. Twenty per cent of anything will produce 80 per cent of the results. So focus on the top five things each day, each week, each month and each year – then do them!

Adrian Geering

Rule One – the customer is always right. Rule Two – refer to Rule One.
Roger Drake

You can't rely on everyone. Occasionally, some will let you down. Don't blame them; look at how you manage and communicate with them. Continually check in on people to see how they're going.

Chris Stathy

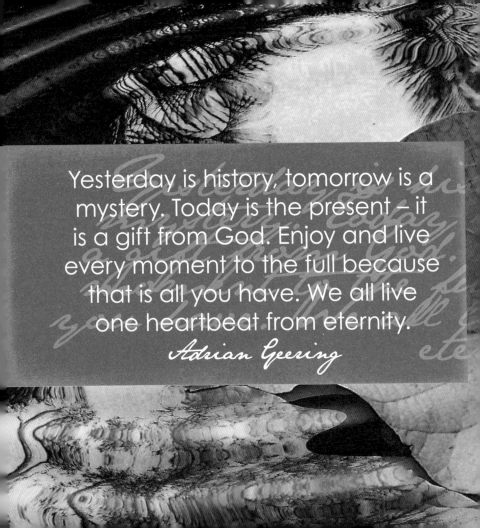

Talk with your staff. Give them plenty of training, information and the tools they need to get the job done with precision.

Scott Hicks

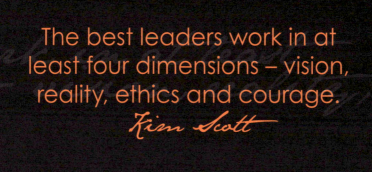

> The best leaders work in at least four dimensions – vision, reality, ethics and courage.
> *Kim Scott*

Have the self-belief to try new things, the passion to persist and the flexibility to know when to let go.

Anthony Foop

The future belongs not to those who know how to make things, but to those who know how to sell things. In other words, success is no longer about production - it's about marketing and distribution.

Bob Day

Also by Adrian Geering ...
Secrets of successful
CEOs

Insights into life, leadership and business

Secrets of Successful CEOs is an insightful, inspiring and elegant book on the dynamic role of the CEO. Written by leading Australian and internationally recognised mentor and business coach, Adrian Geering, it presents extraordinary insights into the lives, leadership and businesses of 20 CEOs.

Are you ready for a mind shift? Are you ready to start thinking like a successful CEO and reap the rewards on offer? *Secrets of Successful CEOs* unlocks the "art of the possibility" to harness the potential in your life, to achieve greatness as a leader and to facilitate the leverage of your business. Full of wisdom, great suggestions and insightful tips.

www.secretsofceos.com